STRENGTH TRAINING FOR SOCCER

Ralf Meier

Strength Training for Soccer

MEYER & MEYER SPORT

Original title: Krafttraining für Fußballer
© Meyer & Meyer Verlag, 2006
Translated by Heather Ross

British Library Cataloguing in Publication Data
A catalogue record for this book is available from the British Library

Ralf Meier
Strength Training for Soccer
Oxford: Meyer & Meyer Sport (UK) Ltd., 2007
ISBN 978-1-84126-208-6

© 2007 by Meyer & Meyer Sport (UK) Ltd.
Aachen, Adelaide, Auckland, Budapest, Graz, Johannesburg,
New York, Olten (CH), Oxford, Singapore, Toronto
Member of the World
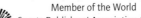 Sports Publishers' Association (WSPA)
www.w-s-p-a.org
Printed and bound by: B.O.S.S Druck und Medien GmbH, Germany
ISBN: 978-1-84126-208-6
E-Mail: verlag@m-m-sports.com
www.m-m-sports.com

Foreword

There is more to the modern game of soccer than just kicking a ball around. Even at the grass roots level, fighting ability, athleticism and agility often make the difference between victory and defeat. This book shows you how to take your athletic performance to the next level and disproves the theory that targeted strength training makes players slow and inflexible. The opposite is actually the case, as you need strength to be fast. Strong leg muscles ensure that when it comes to the crunch, you can get to the ball more quickly than your opponent on the ground and in the air. Well-conditioned leg muscles also give you an advantage in difficult tackles.

Joints, tendons and ligaments are particularly vulnerable on the soccer pitch, and strains, meniscus problems and tendonitis are a fact of life for the soccer player. The best way of protecting the passive musculoskeletal system against potential injury is with strong muscles. This book shows you how to incorporate the right strength training exercises into your training program.

Good luck!
Ralf Meier

Contents

ATHLETICISM IN SOCCER

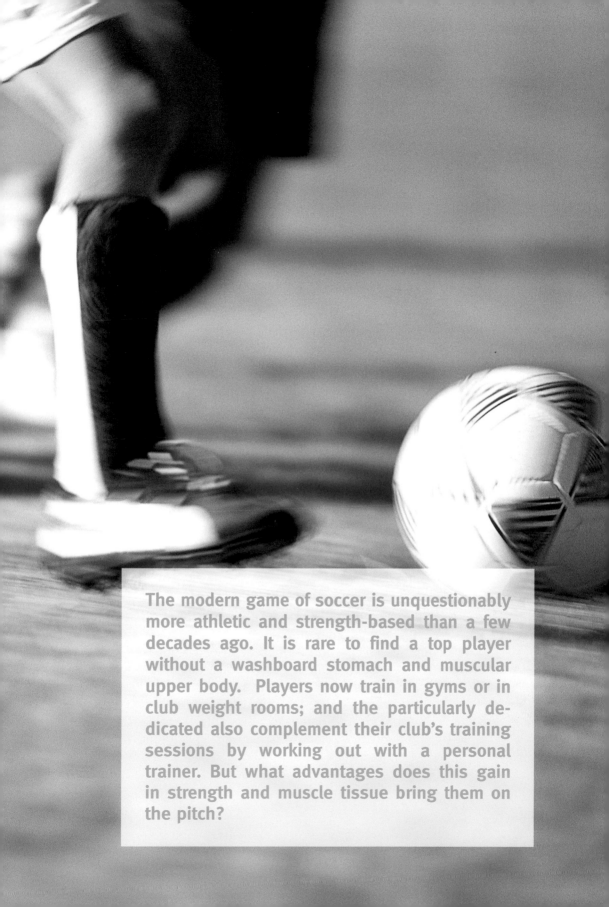

The modern game of soccer is unquestionably more athletic and strength-based than a few decades ago. It is rare to find a top player without a washboard stomach and muscular upper body. Players now train in gyms or in club weight rooms; and the particularly dedicated also complement their club's training sessions by working out with a personal trainer. But what advantages does this gain in strength and muscle tissue bring them on the pitch?

Well-developed muscles reduce the risk of injury. Even in the fairest of games, which are few and far between these days anyway, a certain amount of physical contact is unavoidable. It is not surprising then that soccer is consistently one of the highest risk sports.

The risk of injury does not deter die-hard soccer players, nor should it. The right preparation can significantly reduce the risks of the game.

Training Tip

A strength training warm-up should involve moving as much muscle mass as possible by running on the treadmill or cycling on the ergometer. Jumping on a minitrampoline is a good low-impact alternative. Stretching has no place in the warm-up phase, as it is dangerous for "cold" muscles. Instead you can do one or two warm-up sets with light weights before increasing the load to your training weight.

As well as giving a high level of general physical fitness, the main benefit of well-trained muscles is the prevention of injuries. In the normal loads that occur during a game, such as tackles, twisting or abrupt stops, it is the strength of the muscles surrounding the passive musculoskeletal system that determine whether it is damaged by these stresses or it can absorb and harmlessly dissipate them. Muscles support and protect vulnerable structures like joints, tendons and ligaments.

The key to good physical preparation is a warm-up before the workout or the game.

Of course, they have their limits. If you prefer to follow fashion and roll your socks down around your ankles, instead of pulling them up over your shin pads, you should not be surprised if you end up with your leg in plaster. In addition, few soccer players are as lucky as their professional counterparts to be able to play on manicured pitches, and must instead run about on muddy fields that only resemble soccer pitches in their dimensions.

PROBLEM AREAS

The key to good physical preparation is a warm-up before the workout or the game. Well warmed-up muscles are better able to absorb the leverage and rotational forces that often act on the joints and ligaments during the game.

By far the most complicated joint of all, the knee, is most commonly affected. In soccer, it is often subjected to enormous stress. Severe, acute knee problems are not usually directly caused by opponents, but by awkward rotational forces and leverage forces that can occur if the foot gets caught up in the turf or in an opponent's leg after a kick. Even a normal kick can cause problems for the knee joint and surrounding ligaments. Well-trained and well warmed-up muscles offer protection from serious injuries.

In the knee area, the key is well-developed quadriceps muscles and hamstring muscles, which can be achieved by including exercises on the leg extension and leg curl machines in your training program. It is important to train the muscles through their whole range of movement and to complement strength training with stretching right from the start. Intensive strength training increases muscular tension, which can cause new problems if it not dealt with. Powerful but shortened thigh muscles increase the risk of injury.

Exercise on the leg extension and leg curl machines strengthen the muscles at the front and back of the thigh that are so important for soccer players.

ACHILLES TENDONS

It is not just the knees that are subject to great stress in soccer. The ankle is also vulnerable. Soccer players often complain about significant pain in this area, while injuries in the lower ankle (between the tarsal bones and the ankle bone) are significantly rarer than those in the upper ankle (between the ankle bone and the bones of the lower leg) and are usually caused by sprains affecting the outside of the foot.

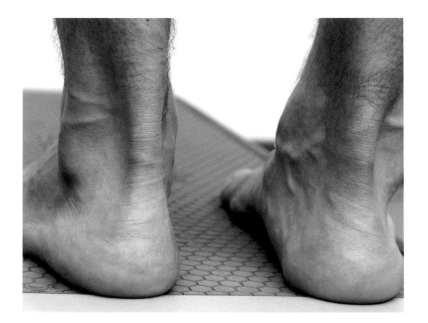

With increasing muscular degeneration, Achilles tendon problems also increase, even leading to tears. The old rule holds true: make sure that injuries are completely healed before resuming training. In the acute stages of inflammation, icepacks are the best treatment. In the long term, the targeted strengthening of the calf muscles is the best protection against further problems. Tendon tears are usually caused by asymmetrical loads due to incorrect foot placement and by shortened calf muscles. Adequate stretching and strengthening exercises ensure the long-term offloading of the tendons and freedom from injury.

Stretching and strengthening exercises aid the long-term offloading of the Achilles tendons.

Professional players can rely on a whole team of doctors, physio-therapists and coaches when they suffer from Achilles problems, who work hand in hand on the physical condition of their protégé. Amateur players often feel that they are left to deal with their pain alone.

Coaches and physicians initially advise complete rest until the injury improves. If one dares to return to training after a few apparently injury-free months, the tendonitis often comes back.

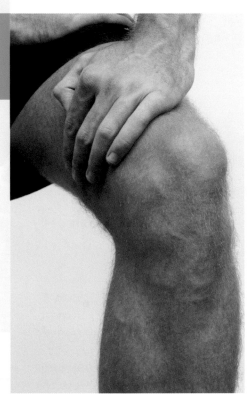

Stretching and strengthening exercises are important for calves and Achilles tendons.

The reason is clear: the tendonitis is not caused by playing soccer, but by weak calf muscles. Until they are strengthened; the tendons will always be overloaded. Worse still: the enforced rest will have weakened the calf muscles even more, and made them even less able to offload the tendons. Anyone who has ever had to deal with this kind of problem before knows how irksome stubborn inflammations in this area can be. At times, one doesn't even dare to put one's weight on the foot concerned anymore.

THE MUSCLES

First on the list of areas particularly vulnerable to soccer injuries are the muscles themselves. Nearly one third of all injuries involve muscles. This ranges from harmless muscle stiffness due to unusually high training loads, via bruises and strains, to complete muscle or fiber tears. The best protection against all of these is a thorough pre-workout or pre-game warm-up and targeted strength training.

Strength is the pre-requisite for every kind of movement. Contrary to the commonly held view, bigger and stronger muscles do not slow you down. Strong muscles are always quick muscles, too. Weightlifters and the like are always excellent sprinters. Anyone who wants to improve their sprinting does not need to run more; they need to improve the maximal strength of their thigh muscles.

Training Tip

In many sports, athletes work on their maximal strength in the winter. In soccer, it makes more sense to shift this intensive phase to the summer. While your teammates need longer to get back in shape after the break, you will surprise everyone with your improved sprinting form.

To be sure, more and more soccer players are using gyms and training machines, although they do usually choose relatively light weights and high reps. This only makes sense though if their main goal is local muscle endurance, which is already one of the core elements of soccer training. Time-consuming "pumping iron" increases neither speed, jumping ability nor explosiveness.

Weight training for soccer must be intensive and heavy. Maximal strength training means no more and no less than loads that regularly approach current performance limits, in order to raise them. The weights lifted should be at least 85% of the max. For weights this heavy, the number of reps is limited to 3-5 at most. Great concentration is needed to lift weights this heavy, and this weight paired with increasing fatigue levels make it a real challenge for the central nervous system. In the long term, maximal strength training not only increases speed and strength, it also makes peak performance available almost on demand.

Maximal strength training means regularly raising one's performance limits.

Soccer players should work out with heavy weights and low reps – this is the ideal way to weight train.

The training is only done periodically during the season. Even then, 2-3 relatively short training sessions per week are quite enough. Maximal strength should only be worked on once the core trunk muscles are strong enough to be able to stabilize the spine during high loads. Maximal training is followed by phases in which the attained strength level is stabilized and recovery phases. There will be more on this later.

Training Tip

If you don't know what you can do, you are leaving your training results more or less to chance. That is why you should check your maximal strength at regular intervals. Your training weight can then be calculated according to this value.

STRENGTH TRAINING FOR SOCCER

SQUATS

Heavy full squats are the most effective exercise that weight training has to offer. They load both the front and back of the thigh. The calf muscles are held static. The knee joint is moved through almost its entire range of movement, so that strengthening stimuli work on the surrounding structures (muscles, tendons) in every position of the joint. Correctly performed squats also represent the most natural load for the whole body. The key point for soccer players is that the functional strengthening of the leg muscles offloads problem areas like the knees and the Achilles tendons.

The full squat mainly affects the quadriceps muscles, i.e., the large leg extensor muscles on the front of the thigh. The buttock muscles and the biceps femoris muscle (hamstring) at the back of the thigh are also involved. In the case of heavy squats, the lower back muscles also play a supporting role and should therefore be warmed up before performing squats. Because of the number of muscles involved, the squat requires great coordination, but this is also what makes it so beneficial.

Full squats require great concentration.

The effectiveness of the exercise also depends on the heaviness of the weight used. For example, if a 75 kg athlete squats with 150 kg on his shoulders, his feet carry a total of 225 kg! There is also a psychological advantage. In hardly any other exercise is the battle against the bar and weights so clear-cut and exciting, creating an incomparable training motivation and aggression that is necessary to voluntarily lift such high loads.

EXECUTION

A pre-requisite for heavy squats is a stable barbell rack, with variable bar rests, if possible. Then lift the bar from the stand with the shoulders. To avoid pressure points, pull the shoulders back a little as you do so, so that the bar's support area is as wide as possible and pressure on the spine is reduced. It is a good idea to cushion the bar with well-developed trapezius muscles or a piece of foam. Then grip the bar with both hands and take one step back from the stand.

> To avoid pressure points, pull your shoulders back when squatting with a barbell.

If you have ever had the feeling of falling backward in a squat position when squatting without weights because you have to raise your heels from the floor, you would do well to use a pair of disk weights or a piece of wood under your heels for stability. An even better idea though is to make sure that your calf muscles are stretched long enough to start with so that you can adopt a squat position without needing to use a wedge. It is best to experiment without a bar until you are able to adopt a stable squat position.

Place your feet about should-width apart – your feet should point slightly outwards – and bend your knees. How deep you squat naturally depends on your training goal. If you just want to improve your jumping strength with this exercise, you can do "quarter squats." This enables you to work with enormous loads because the thigh muscles in this area can generate a great deal of strength. However, the full functionality of the muscles is lost though, because the downward movement stops when the thighs are parallel to the floor. This downward movement must be stopped using muscle strength and not by bouncing the knees. Giving or sagging at the knees can be dangerous for the ligaments and joints in the knee and for the lower back.

The upward movement that follows can present considerable dangers for the hips and spine. To reduce the load on the hips and vertebral disks, make sure that you don't round your back. The bar should only be pushed up using the strength of your legs, as far as possible. Look ahead throughout the movement. As you begin, it can help to watch yourself in a mirror. As you increase the load, you must be able to feel when your body is in the right position. Better still is holding the bar in front of your neck so that it rests on your shoulders, for a front squat. However, this exercise takes a lot of getting used to and is not suitable for beginners. In order to stabilize yourself during the exercise, a spotter is recommended. In the case of very high loads, two training partners are required, one at each end of the bar.

A training partner should act as spotter during the exercise for safety reasons.

Medical Tip

Especially for older players, there is a very important side-effect of strength training: increased muscle tissue is also beneficial for general fitness. Fat and glucose metabolisms are boosted, and the more muscles you have, the easier it is for you to control your weight.

In Focus

MUSCLE FUNCTION TEST

In the planning of a meaningful strength training program, existing deficiencies must be identified by using the so-called muscle function test. Are any muscles shortened or too weak? What is the strength ratio between agonist and antagonist? Are there any asymmetries, limited movements or even joint misalignments?

The answers to these questions determine the structure of the training program and the choice of exercises. For instance, in the case of a knee joint misalignment, it can be a good idea to start off by focusing on strengthening certain parts of the quadriceps – either the vastus medialis, which arises from the inside of the knee, or the vastus lateralis on the outside. This depends entirely on whether the player is bow-legged or knock-kneed. Ignoring these defective positions at the start of the training process could have disastrous consequences.

But a few more potentially serious weaknesses must also be considered before starting to lift heavy weights. A good coach can use a muscle function test to get a good overview of the condition of your musculoskeletal system, and even identify weaknesses, in a few moments.

These weaknesses include shortened muscles, which can be caused by one-sided movement patterns or decreasing muscle strength. This means that a joint's natural range of movement will be limited by a particular muscle. Very often, this can be seen in the problem most beginners have in keeping the entire soles of their feet on the floor when squatting. This is caused by shortened calf muscles. The natural range of movement easily allows this position. Watch little children playing, they can crouch for hours in this position.

For the soccer player, it is particularly interesting if such weaknesses appear in the lower limbs. As well as the calf muscles, the hamstrings, hip flexors and adductors are often affected. In the upper body, it is often the chest, trapezius and the hand and wrist extensor muscles.

SUMMARY

- Soccer is one of several sports with the highest injury rates

- Muscle injuries account for a third of all soccer injuries

- Strong muscles significantly reduce the risk of injury

- Greater strength increases speed, jumping ability and explosiveness

- Strength training for soccer must be intensive and heavy

- Muscles must always be worked out through their entire range of movement

Performance Impr

vement

Is it just a myth that too many muscles lead to stiffness and lack of flexibility? Yes and no! It depends entirely on what kind of training you do. Many hobby athletes do find that years of weight training actually lead to a loss of flexibility. There are very few top weightlifters who cannot easily do splits though, and the "big" guys now really have the kind of thigh circumference that one rarely finds even in body building gyms.

Does strength training make a person slow and inflexible? It's like asking, is my car less nippy if I give the engine more horsepower? Of course not. Acceleration and top speed both benefit from the improved power.

This is true for nearly all sports, not just soccer. Since coaches have lost the negative image they had of strength training, performances everywhere have really gone through the roof. This is quite obvious in events like sprinting, where top male and female athletes typically have well-defined muscles.

Since coaches lost their negative image of strength training, performances have really gone through the roof.

Don't be deceived though. Strength is not always so easily visible. In the lower weight classes of weightlifters and powerlifters, one finds athletes whose muscles betray nothing of the performances of which they are capable.

Whether the trained muscles bulge out or not is partly genetically conditioned and partly dependent on the amount of body fat. On no account should you be afraid that you will need to buy a new wardrobe of clothes after a few training sessions. If it were that simple to build up muscle tissue, the worl-dwide problem of doping would not exist at its current level.

You will actually see that it is not so easy to stimulate muscle growth exactly where you want it.

Training Tip

Training with weights does more than increase strength and muscle tissue, it also causes calluses on the hands. The safest way to prevent the formation of calluses is to wear training gloves. The gloves should fit tightly so that they don't slip while you are lifting.

But if an increase in strength makes one quicker, why did even successful coaches not allow their protégés to train with weights for decades?

This question is not so easy to answer. For a long time, the attitude of the coach was strongly affected by public opinion. In Europe, the first great boom in strength sports took place at the end of the 19th century. The athletes of the time were perceived to be freaks, not athletes, who displayed their strength in fairs or in vaudeville. "Real" athletes naturally wanted nothing to do with this kind of exhibitionism.

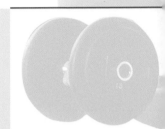

The first strength sport athletes were not considered to be true sportsmen by the general public.

Although strength played an important even back in the ancient Olympic games, this aspect was ignored for a long time in modern sport. The same is also true for science. All aspects of endurance have been thoroughly investigated in countless studies, but almost nothing was known about the development of strength. In sport, as elsewhere, ignorance has been the natural breeding ground for prejudice.

Strength is now generally acknowledged to be a performance-determining factor in sports.

BOOST YOUR GAME

Nowadays, strength is universally acknowledged to be a performance-determining factor in sports. Whether or not additional strength training actually improves your performance depends on the training program used. In any case, the body does not adapt to new, higher loads during the workout, but in the recovery phase that follows. As for the overwhelming majority of soccer players, for whom the sport is "only" a hobby, both the sequencing and structure of the workouts must be well planned.

Training Tip

Up to now, the commonly held view has been that only regular endurance training is beneficial for the cardio-vascular system. In an appropriate workout, e.g., in the form of a circuit, strength training can also have physiological (affecting function) and morphological (affecting size) benefits for the heart.

Continual improvement in performance is what training is all about. This means the adaptation of the body to the demands of training, i.e., increased heart and muscle size or improved muscular coordination. The desired growth of muscles and strength can only be achieved when the frequency and intensity of the training stimuli force the muscles to adapt. Only if the mix of training loads, the fatigue they cause and the ensuing recovery phase are optimally coordinated can the so-called **supercompensation** effect take place.

For this to happen, the body must be able to refill its energy reserves after the workout in which it has lost energy potential and become fatigued, and not just to the starting level but considerably above this level. It is as though the body is preparing itself for further anticipated loads by getting stronger.

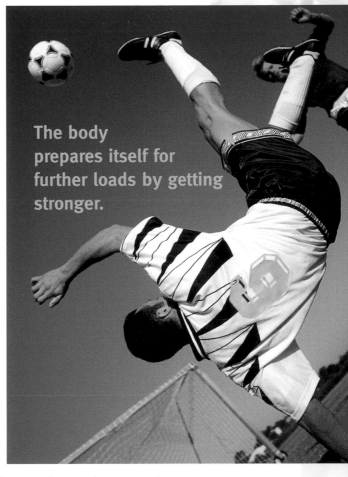

The body prepares itself for further loads by getting stronger.

This supercompensation does not actually last for long. An essential secret of every targeted training program lies in locating the next workout during this phase so as to reach the next supercompensation level.

The supercompensation levels depend on the athlete's training condition, age, gender, motivation, physiology and training content. A generalization about when the supercompensation peak is reached in any given sport, and therefore about how frequently one has to train, is not possible. Experienced athletes often rely on how their body feels or on their coach's experience.

However, in general, training theory states that the supercompensation curve for endurance is steeper than that for strength. This means that to improve endurance performance, you need to work out more often during the week (2-3 times) to develop strength. One intensive, hour-long strength workout per week can, in recreational sport at least, lead to clear improvements in muscle strength.

A well-planned training program aims to reach the next supercompensation level.

It is always more effective to spread strength training over several workouts during the week.

In any case, it is even more effective to spread out your strength training workouts throughout the week, i.e., if you have 2 hours to spend on strength training, it is better to do 2 x 1-hour, or better still 4 x 30-minute workouts per week. However, the individual workouts should not be so short that there is no time to tire the muscles.

Medical Tip

Strength training presents the body with quite different demands than team or endurance sports. When training with heavy weights, there can be very high peaks of blood pressure. It is essential that those suffering from high blood pressure discuss their training program with a physician first.

THE RECOVERY FACTOR

As mentioned above, top soccer players have a whole entourage looking after their well-being. But even amateur players help themselves recover more quickly between workouts. To be really effective, a training program must allow for optimal recovery between workouts. Otherwise, there is a danger of overtraining, causing such effects as loss of performance, higher risk of injury, aversion to training, etc.

There are several stages to the recovery process. The training load more or less exhausts the body's energy reserves. These energy reserves are replenished during the recovery phase. An important part of this process is the ability to break down accumulated metabolites, such as lactic acid, to enable the anabolic processes to begin. The energy required for this is obtained from the "powerhouses" of the muscles, the mitochondria. The better the energy supply within the muscle, the faster the recovery process will take place.

ACTIVE OR PASSIVE

There are a whole range of ways of encouraging recovery after working out. Active recovery methods are preferable, and ideally they should directly follow the workout.

Low intensity physical activities, like stretching, aid recovery.

Medical Tip

A bath taken for recovery purposes should be hotter than 37°C. This stimulates the peripheral blood supply and accelerates the breakdown of waste products accumulated during training. Combined with circulation-boosting bath products, it is an ideal and valuable way of switching off physically and mentally after exercise.

Russian research, in particular, has shown that deliberately low intensity sporting activity has an extremely positive effect on recovery. The nervous system is gently shifted from load to recovery, the breakdown of waste products is considerably accelerated and energy-supply processes are gradually returned to "normal." Gentle jogging or stretching exercises are particularly recommended. The cool-down should last for 10-20 minutes, depending on the length of the preceding workout. Passive methods, such as sauna, ultrasound or hot baths, round off the program. In practice, these methods are used only rarely though, for most amateur players do nothing to aid post-workout recovery. This means that despite increasing training volume, these players rarely attain the success they are looking for.

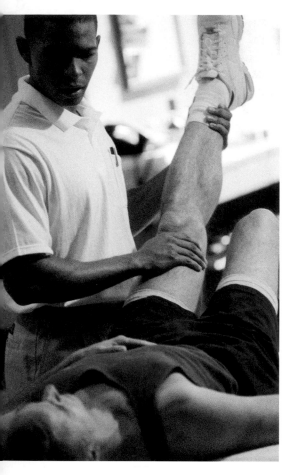

Experienced masseuses know after a few touches which muscles need relaxing first.

Hardworking muscles appreciate an expert massage. For recreational athletes who do more than 2 or 3 light workouts per week, regular muscular relaxation is so important that, at least during intensive training phases, it should be performed twice a week. A less-expensive partial massage is usually sufficient and an experienced masseur can tell after a few touches which muscle groups are so tense that they need priority treatment.

Recreational athletes should also relax their muscles thoroughly after an intensive workout.

Sports massage is more widely available than therapeutic massage. Elementary techniques for both massage types are stroking, rubbing, kneading, tapping and percussing. Sports massage also deals with the joints, as well as the muscles.

The formation of synovial fluid is stimulated, thus reducing wear and tear. The increase in blood flow increases the skin's elasticity and supplies more oxygen to the organs. That, in turn, has a positive effect on the carbohydrate, protein and fat metabolism, and even benefits cholesterol levels. Metabolites are removed more quickly and recovery between workouts is faster.

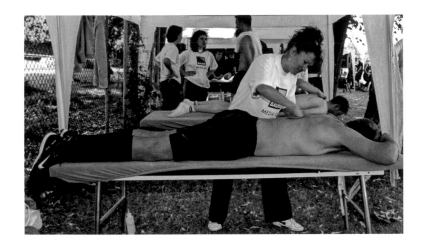

Sports massage is more widely available than therapeutic massage.

Medical Tip

In intensive training phases, myogeloses can form. These are small, tangible, areas of hardening in the muscle that can be quite painful. Although they are small, they affect the elasticity of the muscle as a whole. In the initial stages, they can usually be broken down by a hot shower jet, but stubborn myogeloses must be removed by massage.

In Focus

IS IT POSSIBLE TO OVERTRAIN?

The motto "more is more" is only partly true for the stimuli required for ongoing strength gain. Muscles do not respond to low-level training stimuli, but excessive stimuli, e.g., from training too often, do not produce the desired effect either.

The muscles must be stimulated to grow by the weight during the training process. The response to these stimuli, i.e. muscle growth, only takes place after the workout, in the recovery phase. Depending on training load and performance level, empirical evidence shows that the optimal recovery time is 24-48 hours. The next workout should take place within this timeframe.

For beginners and less experienced players, three-times weekly workouts are sufficient. Only those with competitive ambitions and appropriate levels of physical conditioning should do more. Then, elaborate ways of dividing up training, like the split or double split system, can be used, in which different muscle groups are trained in different workouts in order to give each muscle group a longer recovery despite the increased workout frequency. In the double split system, the daily workout is divided yet again so that one session takes place in the morning and one in the afternoon. This enables more time to be devoted to individual muscle groups. In any case, only those with several years' bodybuilding experience need to use the split or double split systems.

SUMMARY

- More strength makes one faster and more explosive

- Don't worry about your muscles getting too big

- The phenomenon of strength was under-researched for a long time

- Load, fatigue and recovery must all be coordinated

- The magic formula for performance improvement is called supercompensation

Help your body after the workout with active and passive recovery methods

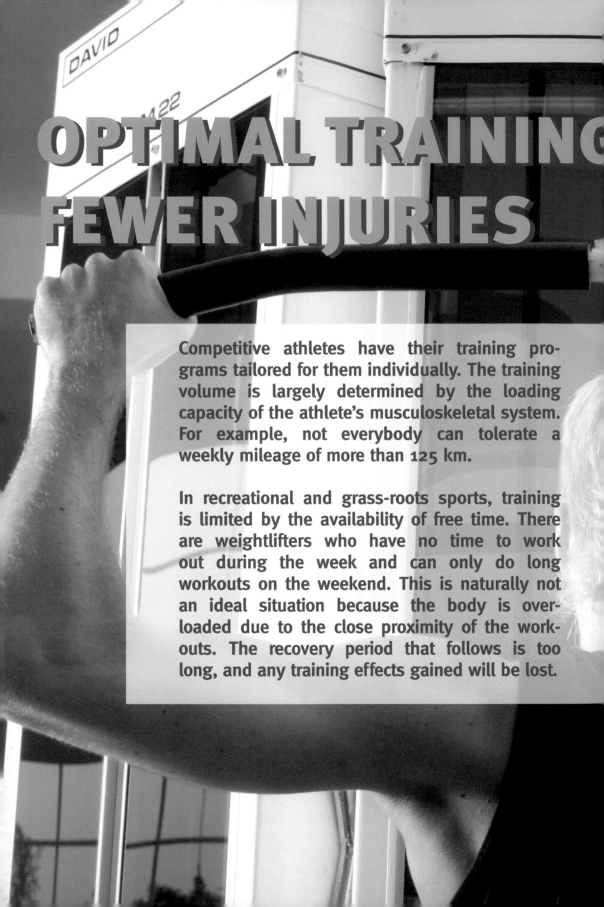

OPTIMAL TRAINING
FEWER INJURIES

Competitive athletes have their training programs tailored for them individually. The training volume is largely determined by the loading capacity of the athlete's musculoskeletal system. For example, not everybody can tolerate a weekly mileage of more than 125 km.

In recreational and grass-roots sports, training is limited by the availability of free time. There are weightlifters who have no time to work out during the week and can only do long workouts on the weekend. This is naturally not an ideal situation because the body is overloaded due to the close proximity of the workouts. The recovery period that follows is too long, and any training effects gained will be lost.

From a statistical point of view, weight training is a low-risk activity, if performed correctly.

From a statistical point of view, weight training in a gym is a relatively low-risk activity. However, if lifts are carried out incorrectly, the risk increases considerably. One has to decide whether the likely benefits outweigh the potential risks.

The risks run by someone who does no sports at all are a great deal higher than the possible health damage due to working out with bars, weights and weight-training machines. The heart attack caused by lack of exercise and stress is hardly comparable to a bout of tendonitis. The comparatively low number of injuries caused by moderate weight training are nearly always due to inadequate warm-ups, loss of concentration while training or performing lifts incorrectly.

An appropriate warm-up, e.g., running on the treadmill, protects against weight training injuries.

IMBALANCES

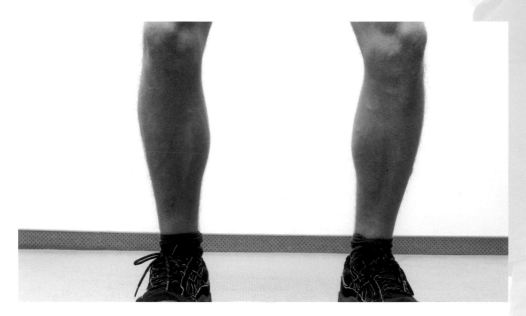

Along with acute externally caused injuries, joint mis-alignments, such as knock-knees and bow-leggedness, and non-symmetrical strength development account for a higher physical injury-proneness. These so-called **muscular disbalances** do not occur by accident and are not usually hereditary but acquired. One-sided loads and overloading are the causes of this phenomenon, which in the most serious cases can end a sporting career. In many racket and team sports, it is usually a leg or a throwing arm that has been used one-sidedly for many years.

The consequences are wide-ranging and can affect joints, the spine, muscles, ligaments or tendons. An important goal of strength training for soccer is also to strengthen the structures that are completely neglected during the game, which strengthens some muscles more than others. These weaker muscles can be built up by targeted weight training, but they disappear again if training ceases. The muscles atrophy if they are underused for a while and they can no longer do their job optimally. This job consists mainly of moving and protecting joints, by moving the joint through

Joint misalignments such as bow-leggedness make the body more injury-prone.

Strength training for soccer targets the structures that are neglected during the game.

its complete range of movement. The worse the condition of your muscles, the less protection there is for the corresponding joint. If there is also a imbalance between the agonist and antagonist, a training session can easily have serious consequences.

But even weighttraining itself can be responsible for non-symmetrical muscular development, such as when training focuses on certain muscles groups and a small number of ex-ercises. Young men in particular like to concentrate on doing bench pres-ses and biceps exercises, thereby neglecting the other parts of the body. Although this does create an impressive physique, it also disturbs the natural strength balance of the body.

Avoid non-symmetrical muscle development. For example, when you train your biceps, don't neglect your triceps.

Training Tip

A weightlifting belt brings mechanical stability to the abdominal area and lower back by increasing the pressure on these areas. It is recommended in those exercises where compressive forces work along or diagonally across the long axis of the body, i.e. especially for squats, but also for shoulder and neck lifts like the inclined bench press.

CORRECTING IMBALANCES

It requires time and patience to bring neglected muscles to the same level as the disproportionately developed ones, but it is worth it. If the discrepancy is particularly great, it can be a good idea to start by focusing on building up the weaker muscles and merely stretching the stronger ones. That is easier said than done though. For example, if the right leg is much stronger and more muscular than the left, it dominates in nearly all two-legged exercises, such as squats. The result of this is that the right leg gets stronger and stronger, but at the same time, the joints in the right leg also work harder. This is pointless, and it would be more beneficial to use leg curl and extension machines on which each leg can be worked separately.

Machines on which each leg can be worked independently help to avoid non-symmetrical muscular development.

GOAL SETTING

Lifting weights twice a week does not make you a weightlifter. You are still a soccer player, who complements his original discipline with weight training. You must therefore use the small amount of time you have available to dedicate to weight training as effectively and usefully as possible. This can only happen if you start off by setting concrete goals and, if possible, can determine the timeframe in which you want to achieve them.

The more time you invest in soccer training, the greater the trade-off will be. You should only do highly intensive maximal strength training periodically during game-free periods. This is especially true for leg training. You cannot do squats near your max weight and then expect to be able to sprint on the pitch a couple of hours later. Heavily loaded muscles need absolute rest in which to regenerate and gain strength. If you deny yourself this rest, you will achieve exactly the opposite result.

Medical Tip

Muscles and tendons must be given the chance to regenerate completely now and then. After each complete training cycle, take a few days off and give yourself a two- to three-week break from weightlifting at least once a year, but without cutting out exercise altogether.

During the season, the goal of weight training is different. It is now about maintaining the higher strength level achieved during the off-season. The muscles do not get stronger; they just don't get any weaker. Luckily, maintenance training is not as arduous as muscle building training. There should still be a certain amount of muscle stimulation, and regularity is essential for every type of training anyway.

STARTING OUT IS EASY

Your body is basically a lazy soul that likes its home comforts. Confront it with a task that challenges it. For example, do 10 reps with a weight that you had previously only lifted 8 times. This allows you to lift the weight with less effort the next time around. The reason for this is the phenomenon of supercompensation described in the previous chapter Unfortunately, this process has its limits, which are relatively low. It quickly becomes a struggle for your muscles to lift each extra kilo added to the bar.

The stronger you get, the more difficult it becomes to progress further.

Medical Tip

When trying to lift heavy weights, there is always the danger of holding one's breath or deliberately trying not to exhale. In extreme cases, the high pressure in the chest area that this causes can stop the flow of blood to the heart. You should therefore concentrate on your breathing to avoid holding your breath.

TRAINING PLANS

Beginners find that in the first weeks of training their strength seems to increase incredibly quickly. But they soon come back down to earth as the rapid increase in strength slows down, and they suddenly start to feel unpleasant twinges in their shoulders and elbows when bench-pressing. This phase decides whether their relationship with weight training is just a brief flirtation or something more long lasting. Many just give up after the first few weeks. Unrealistic expectations, over-training and the resulting aches and pains are the reasons why some people suddenly give up.

An experienced coach and a well-planned training program are the best way to ensure a successful and above all, lasting, relationship with weight training. The rapid strength gain that makes so many beginners prone to overdoing it is only caused by the body becoming used to the lifts. The muscles performing the lifts do not actually get stronger in this short space of time; they just start to work better together. No sooner have you just about got the hang of the lifts, than the rapid strength gain disappears. But only when this phase is over can the real weight training start.

You only really gain strength by increasing muscle size and recruiting as many muscle fibers as possible at the same time. The best way to increase muscle size is to work out with heavy loads (about 75% of max. strength) and 8-12 reps.

Training Tip

The duration of a set is more important than the number of reps. Ten bench press reps can be done in 25 or 45 seconds. In the latter case, the duration of the tension stimulus is longer, and the emphasis is on the development of slow twitch muscle fibers. In the first case, the movements are explosive, which develops speed strength and maximal strength, as well as the growth of fast twitch muscle fibers.

The better trained a muscle is, the more specifically it can control the number of muscle fibers necessary for a lift. With low to average loads it activates fewer fibers than an untrained muscle does, thereby sparing its reserves. With high to maximal loads, it can mobilize up to 95% of all fibers nearly "from cold." Untrained people can barely mobilize half of all the fibers in a muscle, even when lifting heavy weights. The main goal of maximal strength training is to make these inner reserves available.

VARIETY

You need a yearly plan for your weight training just like you do for soccer training. Maximal strength and maintenance training are two forms of weight training.

The third important form is sub-maximal muscle building training. Switching between training in the maximal and sub-maximal zones means that both strength components are mutually developed, making it easier to overcome stagnation in strength development.

Furthermore, the effects of the different weight training methods complement each other, for a muscle consists of numerous different structures, which react to totally different loads. For example, the "white" muscle fibers (fast twitch fibers) like explosive loads, while the "red" (slow twitch) fibers prefer a regular, rather more comfortable rhythm.

Making your training program as varied as possible helps to keep challenging these different muscle elements and provoking them to adapt further. How training can be structured throughout the year and divided into individual workouts is shown in the following chapters.

Support by an experienced coach is the best way of ensuring that you don't give up weight training.

A varied training plan provides a constant challenge for the different parts of a muscle.

In Focus

MUSCLE SORENESS

Muscle soreness, or aching muscles after lifting unfamiliar loads, is something we have all suffered from before, even those who do no sports at all. It is usually caused by lengthening (eccentric or negative) muscle activity, like that involved in running downhill or putting down a heavy weight. After squatting, it is therefore often the muscles of the buttocks and the back of the thigh (m. biceps femoris, etc.) that are affected, although the bulk of the lifting is done by the muscles at the front of the thigh (m. quadriceps). In the case of the bench press, it is usually the chest muscles that are affected, although the bulk of the lifting here is actually done by the arm and shoulder muscles.

The lactic acid hypothesis, which maintains that the cause of muscle soreness is the build-up of lactates in the muscles, is untenable, as this would mean that the muscles doing most of the lifting work would be affected and not the eccentrically loaded muscles that do less work and therefore accumulate less lactic acid. Also going against this hypothesis is the fact that muscle soreness is usually felt some time after the activity that caused it, while the lactate levels are at their peak at the time of highest intensity activity. Nowadays, muscle stiffness is usually attributed to microscopic muscle fiber tears, which are repaired after a few days.

People unused to exercise sometimes find it hard to tell the difference between muscle soreness and a muscle tear. If the pain has not clearly improved after several days, the problem is usually a muscle tear. If you are suffering from muscle soreness, do not train as normal; low intensity activities like loose jogging can help to ease the pain quickly.

SUMMARY

- The injury risk from weight training is low

- Non-symmetrical loads and overloading can cause muscular imbalances

- Beginners tend to overestimate their ability

- Highly intensive maximal strength training phases should only be scheduled during the off-season.

- The stronger you are, the more difficult it is to make further progress

- Less well-trained people can barely activate half of a muscle's fibers even during extreme exertion

SHORT PROGRAM

TO DO AT HOME

Building up muscle tissue does not need to be time-consuming. What matters is the optimal arrangement of the training stimuli. Regular maximal strength tests enable the training weights required at any one time to be determined. You can also easily do the necessary muscle strengthening exercises at home.

To get the most from weight training, you must establish your best performance for each exercise. This maximal strength allows you to structure your workouts most effectively. The following tried and tested guidelines will help you to select the correct training weights.

Low loads are considered to be 30-50% of max. Light is a weight between 50 and 60%. Average is 60-75% and 75-85% is considered to be sub-max. Anything above that falls in the area of maximal weight training. How close to your maximal weight you should train depends on several factors:

- Your training experience

- Your age

- Your physical condition

- Your personal goals

Your training experience is important. Beginners' bodies react to the slightest challenge, so that 40-50% of max is enough for a continual strength gain. After a while, the intensity must be raised to maintain the performance level. You are then training at 75-85% in order to specifically target the growth of muscle tissue where there are still deficiencies. You must work with heavier and heavier weights in order to improve your maximal strength.

Of course, you don't have to work on muscle size. During the playing season, you can work on maintaining the strength you have gained and on recovering from games without too much effort.

In order to maintain your strength, you must gradually increase the weight you lift.

MAXIMAL STRENGTH TEST

In order to always be sure that you are lifting the correct weight, you should definitely carry out a maximal strength test every six weeks or so. As these tests are very taxing for the joints and ligaments, beginners should not undertake them until they have completed a year of regular training. Only then are the muscles required to support loads this heavy sufficiently developed. Young people under the age of sixteen should not attempt them at all.

It is important that you always warm up your muscles well before performing maximal strength tests. Warm up with light weights and then increase the load by a fair amount each time until you reach your current limit. Do three reps each time you increase the load. The aim is just to get a feel for the weights and not to expend too much energy. Maximal strength tests are always separate workouts. There is no point in testing the strength of your leg muscles straight after a normal workout.

If you are able to squat 265 lb with maximal effort and correct technique, this gives the following values for your squats workouts:

- up to 100 lb: Muscle endurance (economizing local metabolic processes)

- 199-225 lb: Muscle growth (building new muscle tissue)

- 225-265 lb: Improving coordination of nerves and muscles (maximal strength training)

Buy yourself a daily training log in which to make a note of all your maximal strength test results. You can only plan your training if you can always keep track of it.

THE SHORT PROGRAM

Soccer is your great passion, but family and work take time. It is probably hard for you to find the time for 2-3 weight training workouts per week on top of the weekly soccer training. One way out of this problem is the short program, which initially enables you to improve and later to maintain your strength. This short program can also be carried out at home. All you need is a training bench and a set of dumbbells. This not only saves you money, but also traveling time to and from the gym.

Medical Tip

As the body loses about 10% of its muscle tissue per decade, regular weight training offers invaluable benefits for senior players. It can help you reduce the risk of injury to your passive musculoskeletal system. Pick up the dumbbells as often as possible to reduce age-related muscle loss.

It is hard to orient yourself to maximal strength targets with a short "at home" program, as they cannot be provided for most exercises. It can be done for dumbbell exercises though. As a beginner, choose weights around 50% of your maximal performance. If you already have weight training experience, choose a load of between 60 and 75%. Many exercises can be done with just your bodyweight.

The short program takes about 45 minutes, including warming up and cooling down. Do the program twice a week on non-consecutive days.

WARMING UP

At the start of the workout, you must warm up all muscle groups to prepare the circulation and the musculoskeletal system for the training program to come.

The most suitable exercises for warming up are those that move as many muscles as possible, for example, running in place for a couple of minutes.

The higher you raise your knees, the harder the exercise is. Try to be as light on your feet as possible so that you don't overload your joints unduly. If you have problems with your ankle or knee joints, buy yourself a minitrampoline for the warm-up phase.

Then do a couple of dynamic loosening exercises. There are no limits to what you can do here. Anything that moves as many muscles as possible is ok. Only static, held stretches are forbidden.

Otherwise, you can do anything from jumping jacks to side bends that you already know from your soccer training warm-up. This will prepare you for your weight training workout in a few minutes.

Squats

1

Place your feet approximately shoulder-width apart with your toes pointing slightly outward. Stretch your arms out in front of you. Lower yourself slowly into a squatting position until your thighs are more or less parallel with the floor. Keep your upper body as straight as possible as you do so and don't round your back.

2
Stand up again, keeping your upper body straigth. Deliberately contract your buttock muscles during the upward movement. This exercise is most effective when carried out slowly and with concentration.

Due to the large amount of muscle mass moved, even the squat with just your bodyweight is one of the most effective strength training exercises you can do. You can vary the exercise by performing it on one leg, in which case you should hold onto something like a door handle for stability.

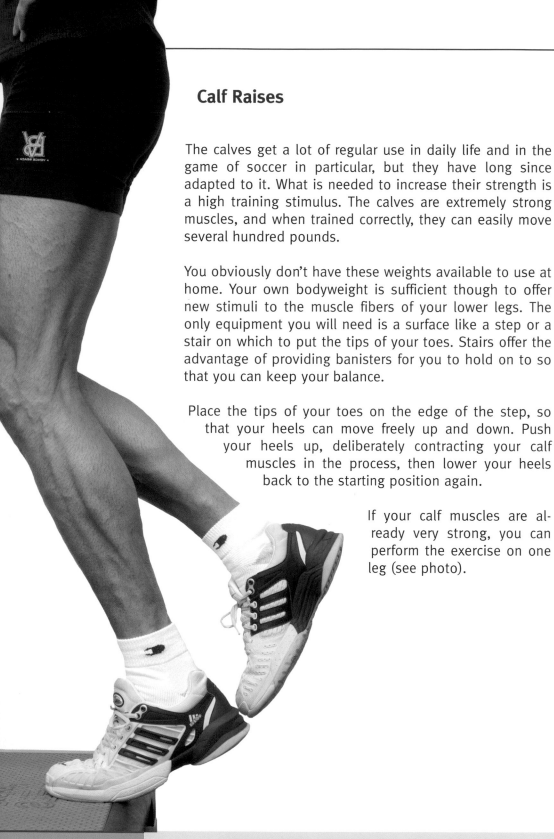

Calf Raises

The calves get a lot of regular use in daily life and in the game of soccer in particular, but they have long since adapted to it. What is needed to increase their strength is a high training stimulus. The calves are extremely strong muscles, and when trained correctly, they can easily move several hundred pounds.

You obviously don't have these weights available to use at home. Your own bodyweight is sufficient though to offer new stimuli to the muscle fibers of your lower legs. The only equipment you will need is a surface like a step or a stair on which to put the tips of your toes. Stairs offer the advantage of providing banisters for you to hold on to so that you can keep your balance.

Place the tips of your toes on the edge of the step, so that your heels can move freely up and down. Push your heels up, deliberately contracting your calf muscles in the process, then lower your heels back to the starting position again.

If your calf muscles are already very strong, you can perform the exercise on one leg (see photo).

Training the Back Extensors

1
Get on all fours, keeping your knees under your hips and your hands under your shoulders. From this position, extend your left arm forward and your right leg backward, with your fingertips pointing forward and your heel pointing backward. This firmly contracts the back, buttock and abdominal muscles. Hold the position for about 10 seconds and then return to all fours.

2
Change sides. Now stretch your right arm to the front and your left leg to the back. Stretch out your neck and look down. Try to keep your balance. Hold the position for about 10 seconds and then return to the starting position.

Pull-Ups between Two Chairs

The back contains a complex network of muscles. These back muscles stabilize the spine and counteract gravity, thereby enabling us to stand up straight. Soccer players in particular often have pronounced muscular imbalances that are detrimental to the upper body. While the thigh muscles tend to be very well-trained, the shoulder and back muscles are usually less so. This muscular imbalance can cause curvatures of the spine and backache.

The back extensors and the muscles responsible for stabilizing the shoulders are usually particularly neglected. One of the most effective exercises for these areas is the pull-up. If you still have a carpet hanger in your backyard, you can even do pull-ups at home. Grip the bar with your hands shoulder-width apart, with your fingers on top. Exhale as you slowly and carefully pull your body up. Your chest should be level with the bar in the final position.

As most people do not possess a carpet hanger, you can make a simple structure at home that will train the same muscles. Place a dumbbell rack (see figure 1) or a stable broomstick (see figure 2) across the backs of two chairs placed so they are facing each other. Lie on the floor on your back between the chairs and grip the bar. Bend your arms, keeping your forearms parallel. Pull your upper body toward the bar. As you do so, deliberately move your shoulder blades toward each other. Then lower your upper body back down onto the floor. As you do the exercise, think of it as a back exercise, not an arm exercise, although your arms are naturally involved.

This exercise is easier than "real" pull-ups, as you do not have to lift your whole bodyweight. However, it provides a good enough work-out for your back extensors and the muscles that stabilize the whole shoulder girdle.

Push-Up

1

Place your hands on the floor slightly more than shoulder-width apart. Rest on the tips of your toes with your feet hip-width apart. Stabilize your core by tensing your abdominal, buttock and back muscles.

2

Bend both arms simultaneously until your upper arms are parallel with your upper body. Then straighten your arms and return to the starting position. If you are not yet strong enough, you can also bend your knees and rest them on the floor instead of resting on your toes.

1

2

Bench Press

If you have a horizontal bench and a set of dumbbells, you can alternate between push-ups and bench press.

1
Lie on your back on the bench and hold a dumbbell in each hand. Open your arms to shoulder-width apart and hold them straight up. Bending your knees and raising your feet will offload your lower back.

1

2

2
Lower the weight carefully toward your chest. Then push the dumbbells up smoothly. Don't hollow your back as you push them up but instead push your lower back into the bench.

Dumbbell Flies

1

Lie on your back on the horizontal bench and hold a dumbbell in each hand. Raise your arms but don't lock your elbows. The palms of your hands are facing each other. Bend your knees and cross your feet.

1

2

Lower the dumbbells to the sides until you feel a clear pull on your chest muscles. Then bring your arms together again. Keep your elbows slightly bent throughout the movement.

2

Crunches

Crunches are the first exercise in your abdominal workout. Lie on your back on the floor or on a mat and bring your hands to your temples. Bend your knees and push your heels firmly against the floor and (at the same time) a little toward your buttocks. This enables you to avoid recruiting the powerful hip flexors, which connect the upper body and trunk across the hip joints.

As you exhale, roll your upper body one vertebra at a time up off the floor. Look diagonally forward, without pushing your chin into your chest. Keep your head relaxed at all times; you are training your abdominals not your neck!

Now lower your upper body one vertebra at a time back down to the floor, without letting your head or shoulders touch the mat. Keep your abdominals contracted throughout the exercise.

Reverse Crunches

While normal crunches mainly develop the area below your navel, this exercise works the muscles above it.

Lie on your back on the floor or on a mat. Raise your legs and bend your knees approximately to right-angles so that your lower legs are now parallel to the floor. As you exhale, slightly lift your bottom off the floor using the strength of your lower abdominal muscles. Then return your pelvis to the floor as you inhale.

You can let your head rest on the floor and stretch your arms out by your sides. Make the exercise more difficult by raising your head from the floor and placing your hands by your temples.

Twisting Crunch

Although the oblique abdominals are also active in exercises for the straight abdominal muscle, it still needs further work. This is particularly true for soccer players, who need a great deal of strength and stability in this area to cope with the high degree of rotational movement when dribbling or tackling.

The starting position for this exercise is the same as for normal crunches. Place your hands at the side of your temples, bend your knees and place your heels on the floor. As you exhale, roll your upper body off the floor, then twist to the side so that your left elbow points toward your right knee in the final position.

Then bring your upper body back to the center again as you inhale, without your head or shoulders touching the floor. Twist your upper body to the other side as you exhale.

OVERVIEW OF THE SHORT PROGRAM

Reps: Smallest strength training unit

Set or Series: Sequence of reps; in conventional weight training, several sets per exercise are carried out with a short rest in between.

Volume: Number of reps in a set, number of sets and number of workouts per week.

Warm-up

Exercise	Time
Running, jumping jacks minitrampoline, cycling on ergometer bike, etc.	10 minutes

Legs

Exercise	Reps	Sets
Two-legged Squats	25	2
One-legged Squats	8-12	3
Calf Raises (One or two-legged)	15-25	3

Back

Exercise	Reps	Sets
Back Extensor	8-10	3
Pull-ups	8-12	3

Chest

Exercise	Reps	Sets
Push-ups	15-25	3-5
Bench Press	12-15	3-5
Flies	10-15	2

Abs

Exercise	Reps	Sets
Crunches	As many as possible	3
Reverse Crunches	As many as possible	3
Twisting Crunches	As many as possible	2

Cool-down

Exercise	Time
Jogging	10 minutes

STRENGTH TRAINING

N THE GYM

The goal of systematic strength training for soccer is not to change the physique or just gain pure strength. It is to provide op-timal preparation for the loads encountered when dealing with the ball and the opponent. Nonetheless, it is still different in the core areas from other strength programs, for soccer players also need to do a lot of work on their upper body, as well as their legs.

Muscle Training for Soccer

The legs naturally need special attention, particularly the muscles surrounding the vulnerable knee joints and the calf muscles. A knee joint that is protected by a strong quadriceps muscle can also absorb adverse loads. The best protection against Achilles tendon problems are again strong and flexible calf muscles. Strong muscles therefore help prevent potential injuries. In addition, increasing the strength of your legs and buttocks always gives you greater explosiveness and speed strength.

The goal of upper body training is above all to stabilize the trunk muscles, with some attention also being paid to the arms. They participate in all pushing and pulling movements in any case. Abdominal, back and bottom muscles are responsible for stabilizing the trunk. You should also strengthen the shoulder stabilizing muscles if you don't want to be knocked out next time you collide with a player on the opposing team. Upper body strength also supports the action of the legs each time you sprint and jump. Appropriate strength can also make up for technical deficiencies when tackling.

Overview

Muscle Groups	Function in Soccer
Legs	Sprinting ability and speed strength, Jumping and shooting strength, protection for knees and ankles
Back/Abdomen	Stabilizing trunk, tackling posture, mobility
Shoulder/neck	Heading dynamics
Arms	Support sprinting and jumping action

Leg Extensions

This exercise enables you to deliberately work on the part of the quadriceps surrounding the knee. If you have the choice in your gym, use a machine that allows you to train each leg separately.

Place your feet about shoulder-width apart on the foot pads. Make sure that the backs of your knees are resting on the knee pad. Press your back firmly against the back of the seat and carefully raise your feet. You can control the effect of the exercise by slightly changing the position of your feet.

Leg Curls

This exercise works the back of the thighs, the hamstrings. In large gyms, there are usually a variety of machines to use. Change machines from time to time. Don't work with a shortened range of movement just so that you can lift heavier weights. Shortened hamstrings reduce your running speed and can also be dangerous for your knee joints.

1
Lie on the cushion with your legs hip-width apart. Make sure that your knee extends beyond the cushion.

1

2
Now pull your heels toward your bottom so that the movement takes place around the knee joint.

2

Squats

Take the barbell from the rack and pull your shoulders back slightly so that the bar lies on your trapezius muscle and not on your cervical spine. Take one step back. Your feet should now be about shoulder-width apart with your toes pointing outward.

1

Go carefully down into a squat position until your thighs are parallel to the floor. Then stand up again, keeping your upper body straight. You need a lot of flexibility to be able to perform the movement correctly. On no account should you round your back during the exercise.

2

If you always lose out when fighting for the ball in the air and already have a year's weight training experience, include quarter squats in your program. This involves stopping the downward movement before your thighs are parallel to the floor and allows you to lift considerably more weight. The exercise develops your jumping ability.

Adductors

There is only one mistake you can make on this machine: increasing the weight too quickly. What other muscles can perhaps forgive can in the case of the adductors involve a lengthy imposed rest. Tears in this area are distinctly unpleasant and painful. So take things slowly.

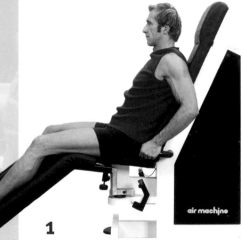

1
Sit on the machine and press your lower back against the back rest. Pull your toes toward you.

1

2
Now carefully bring your legs together. Make sure that it is your inner thigh muscles that instigate the movement.

2

Abductors

The inner and outer thigh muscles are not only responsible for opening and closing the legs. They also stabilize the pelvis during walking and running and are responsible for movements in the hip joint.

Sit up straight against the back rest. Close your legs with the pads against the outside of your legs. Now open your legs as wide as possible. Then carefully bring your legs back together, but without letting the thighs touch each other. Keep your muscles contracted.

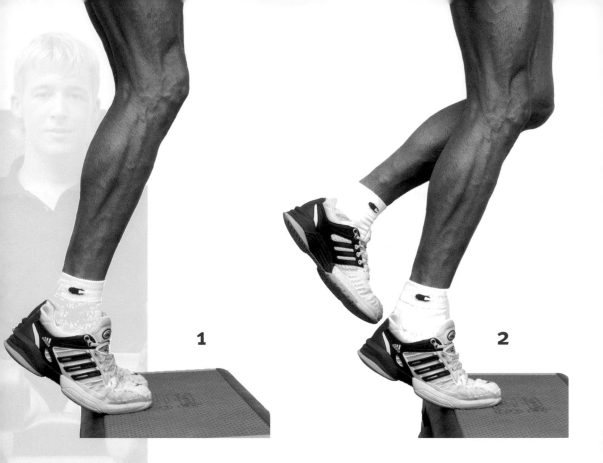

1

2

Calf Raises

1
Stand on the edge of a stepper or a step, so that only the balls of your feet are resting on it and your heels are free to move up and down. Push your heels up while deliberately contracting your calf muscles. Then carefully lower your heels back down to the starting position. You can also hold on to a barbell to help you to keep your balance.

2
If your calf muscles are already very strong, you can also do the exercise on each leg separately.

Leg Kick Backs

This exercise works your gluteus maximus and rear thigh muscles. Strong glutes give you a push when you are sprinting after the ball.

Lay your upper body on the padded cushion, grip the handles at the front with your hands and place your feet on the foot pad behind you. Contract your buttock muscles and push the foot plate hard but carefully backward. The ankle at your knee doesn't change throughout the exercise as the movement comes from your hips.

The exercise can be performed one-legged or two-legged. You can concentrate better on the muscles to be trained when you do it one-legged.

BACK

Lat Pulldowns

1
Sit up straight with a slightly hollowed back on the seat with your feet firmly under the knee pad. Stretch your arms up and grip the bar.

2
Pull the weight down toward the nape of your neck, while moving your shoulder blades down and toward each other. Keep your wrists firm. This exercise should work your back and not your arms. Then carefully return the bar to the starting position.

1

2

Hyperextension

1

Position the apparatus so that your legs can fit comfortably on the pads and your entire upper body sticks out over the end. Contract the muscles of your upper body and fold your arms across your chest.

2

Move your upper body slowly and carefully downward by bending your lower back. As soon as your upper body is parallel to the floor, pause for a moment, then roll back up again. If you have no problems with your spine, you can try to go beyond the horizontal and lower your upper body even further.

You can increase the intensity of the exercise by holding your hands to your temples instead of folding your arms across your chest.

Seated Row

1
Make sure that your upper body is pressed right against the pad and that your back is slightly hollowed. Push your bottom back, push your chest forward and pull your shoulders down and back.

2
Pull the weight toward your body as you exhale, moving your shoulder blades down and together as you do so. Lean your upper body back as you pull. With heavy weights, the support can sometimes hamper breathing, so try to maintain your breathing rhythm.

Bench Press

1

Lie on your back on a horizontal bench and grip the bar a little more than shoulder-width apart. Bend your knees to offload your back. Bring the weight carefully down to the center of your chest.

2

Push the weight up smoothly. Do not hollow your back when the bar is at its highest point.

Inclined Bench Press

This exercise works the same muscle as the bench press, the pectoral muscle, but it also tones the upper fibers in the collarbone area due to the unfamiliar angle. The inclined position also increases the range of motion.

1

1
As with the bench press, grip the bar with your hands a little more than shoulder-width apart and then bring the bar down to the top of your chest. Your elbows should be pointing toward the floor. Keep your wrists firm.

2

Push the weight carefully upward. Your head should continue to rest on the bench.

3

Don't lock your elbows at the highest point. Then carefully lower the bar back to your chest. Avoid hollowing your back in this exercise.

Flies

1

Lie on your back on a bench and bend your knees to protect your lower back. Hold a dumbbell in each hand. Straighten and raise your arms without locking your elbows. The palms of your hands should be facing each other.

1

2

Open out your arms and let your arms fall to the sides until you can feel a clear tug in your pecs. Then carefully bring your arms together again.

2

SHOULDERS

Deltoid Lateral Raise

This exercise targets the neglected lateral and rear areas of the shoulder muscles. It is important that the thumbs point diagonally downward. If the thumbs point up, you will work the front shoulder muscles instead.

1
Stand up straight with your feet hip-width apart. Make sure that you never raise your shoulders during the exercise.

2
Raise your arms to the sides until they are parallel to the floor.
Do not raise them any higher than this.

1

2

Forward Lean Deltoid Lateral Raise

The back of the shoulders is one of the most neglected muscles in weight training. If the other parts of the shoulder get stronger, while the back parts do not, shoulder problems are inevitable.

1
Grip the dumbbells and take one step back. The palms of your hands should face each other. Lean your upper body forward slightly. Make sure that your upper body remains quite stable throughout the movement.

2
Raise your slightly bent upper arms and at the same time, pull your shoulder blades together. In the highest position, your arms should be level with your shoulders. Then carefully lower your arms again.

Behind the Neck Press

In most gyms, there are machines for this exercise, but during a strength cycle you should also do it with dumbbells and barbell.

1
Grip the dumbbells and bend your arms. Hollow your back slightly and contract your stabilizing muscles throughout the set. Make sure that your wrists are firm and don't give way.

1

2

2
Push the dumbbells up. Don't lock your elbows. Then bring the weights back to the starting position.

Barbell Curl

This exercise offers a great range of variations. You can use a straight bar or a curved, so-called EZ Curl bar (see photo). If you suffer from wrist problems, you should always use an EZ curl bar anyway.

1

Stand with your feet hip-width apart and grip the bar.

2

Bring the bar slowly and carefully toward your chest by raising your forearms.

1

2

Pull-Ups with Undergrip

This exercise really works both sides of the biceps hard. The overhead position of the arms means that there is a very strong pre-stretch. Initially, you will have your work cut out just lifting your own bodyweight.

1
Grip the bar with a shoulder-wide undergrip so that your fingers are pointing upward, and the palms of your hands are facing your face. Bend your elbows slightly.

2
Exhale as you pull your body up. In the final position, your chest is level with the bar. Then slowly and carefully lower your body again.

Dumbbell Curls

Stand with your feet hip-width apart and hold a dumbbell in each hand. Now raise your forearms, either both together or each arm alternately.

By beginning the curling action with your hands facing inward at the lowest point and then turning them up as you raise them, this exercise allows you to specifically target the outward twisting movement of your forearm.

Curls on the Machine

This involves training on a support that stops your arms moving backward during the exercise. The grip is usually the same as that for the EZ bar.

1
Hold the bar with both hands. Keep your wrists firm throughout the exercise. Pull the bar toward your upper body.

2
Extend your arms and bring them forward slowly and carefully.

TRICEPS

Narrow Grip Bench Press

The triceps is the antagonist of the biceps and lies at the back of the upper arm. It is a particularly strong muscle that can usually bear considerably higher loads that its better-known counterpart.

1

Lie on your back on a bench and bend and raise your legs to offload your lower back. Hold the bar with an overgrip so that the backs of your hands are facing your head. Your hands should be a little less than shoulder width apart.

2

Push the bar up. Your upper arms shouldn't face the side but rather your elbows should still be shoulder-width apart. Don't lock your elbows.

Dips

1
Support yourself on the dip bars.

2
Let yourself drop slowly and carefully until your upper arms are approximately parallel to the floor. The elbows point backwards and should not drift outward during the movement. Then push up smoothly from the lowest position back to the starting position.

To make the load on the triceps as high as possible, the upper body should be kept upright. If you bend your upper body forward, the chest muscles start to participate in the exercise.

Triceps Press Down

1

Stand next to the stack and take one step back. Hold the bar handles.

2

Pull the bar down. Keep your upper arms next to your body throughout. Only your forearms move up and down. Alternate between all the available handles and cables for the apparatus.

Crunches

Lie on your back on a mat and bring your hands to your temples. Bend your knees and push your heels firmly against the mat. Push your heels slightly toward your bottom. This largely helps to stop the powerful hip flexor muscles from participating in the exercise.

Roll your upper body up from the mat one vertebra at a time. Look straight ahead without pressing your chin into your chest. Relax your head and your neck muscles. Then roll back down one vertebra at a time without letting your head and shoulders touch the mat. Keep your abdomen tense and repeat the movement. Exhale as you raise your upper body and inhale as you lower it.

THE PROGRAMS

Choose your gym carefully, for you can only keep your motivation going when you feel comfortable and well-treated. The more injuries your knees and ankles have suffered in the preceding years, the more important it is to offload these structures with strong muscles until well into your old age. And who knows: perhaps you will lay the foundations in the gym for your sporting activity after your soccer-playing days are over.

At the very least, the large muscles should perform as wide a variety of lifts as possible. This is only possible with a varied training plan. There is little point in only doing the basic weight training exercises (multi-jointed exercises like squats or bench press), as they only work a certain part of the muscle fibers.

The deadlift is one of the basic weightlifting exercises.

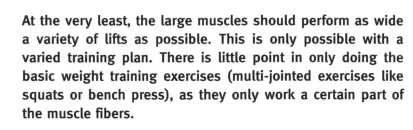

Varying the exercises ensures as comprehensive a workout as possible for the muscles. For example, the inclined bench press also trains the upper fibers of the pecs near the region of the collarbone. If you only do the normal bench press, you will not benefit from this strengthening effect.

It is not only the exercises that need to be varied, but also the order in which they are performed. Your workout should change a little after eight weeks at the most to avoid stagnation and allow for continual improvement. You should therefore alternate muscle building and maximal strength phases to vary training volume and intensity. You can also exchange exercises for certain muscle groups or change the exercise order for a while. This brings variety to your load profile.

STRENGTH TRAINING FOR SOCCER

RANGE OF MOVEMENT

In every exercise, bones move together and apart again. How far apart they move depends on the range of movement of the joint in question. Flexible muscles enable you to use your full range of movement. That is a prerequisite for you to be able to lift the training weight through the full range of motion. If this doesn't happen, the muscles will get stronger in the areas where training is focused due to the restricted movement. A muscle that is only partially strengthened will, in time, lose flexibility.

Go through the full range of movement in every exercise.

Training Tip

Perform all reps at a moderate pace. The basic rule is you should be able to move the weight under control throughout the movement. Of course this doesn't mean you should train In slow-motion, but neither should you train so fast that centrifugal force makes it harder for you to control the weights.

Do not push for the last inch when you perform a lift, i.e., the complete locking of the joints. The benefits here are not worth the long-term risks. The reason many athletes don't use the full range of movement is mainly because the weights they lift are too heavy. It makes absolutely no sense to perform an exercise incorrectly just to be able to lift another 10 lb. This is particularly true for soccer players, who are not trying to break gym records, but just trying to play better on the soccer pitch.

Beginner's Program

Duration:	6-8 weeks
Goals:	Quick learning of the movement forms
	Core stability
Workout Duration:	75-80 minutes

Warm-up

Exercise	Time
Any Cardio Machine	10 mins

Legs

Exercise	Reps	Sets
Leg Extensions	15-25	2
Leg Curls	15-25	2
Adductors	15-25	2

Back

Exercise	Reps	Sets
Hyperextensions	15-25	2
Seated Row	15-25	2

Chest

Exercise	Reps	Sets
Bench Press	15-25	2
Flies	15-25	1

Shoulders

Exercise	Reps	Sets
Lateral Deltoid Raise	15-25	2

Triceps

Exercise	Reps	Sets
Triceps Press Down	15-25	2

Biceps

Exercise	Reps	Sets
Dumbbell Curl	15-25	2

Calves

Exercise	Reps	Sets
Calf Raise	15-25	2

Abdomen

Exercise	Reps	Sets
Crunches	As many as possible to exhaustion	3
Reverse Crunches	As many as possible	2

Cool-down

Exercise	Time
Any Cardio Machine	10 minutes

Muscle Building Training

Duration:	8 weeks; following the Beginner's Program
Loading:	40-60% of max (1st training year) 60-75% of max (experienced)

1st Week's Training

Warm-up

Exercise	Time
Any Cardio Machine	10-15 minutes

Legs

Exercise	Reps	Sets
Leg Curls or Squats	8-12	3
Leg Extensions	12	2
Abductors	12	2

Back

Exercise	Reps	Sets
Hyperextensions	15-25	2
Seated Row	8-12	2

Chest

Exercise	Reps	Sets
Bench Press	8-12	3
Flies	12	2

Shoulders

Exercise	Reps	Sets
Lateral Deltoid Raise	8-12	2
Fwd Lean Lateral Deltoid Raise	8-12	2

Triceps

Exercise	Reps	Sets
Dips	8-12	2

Biceps

Exercise	Reps	Sets
Pull-ups with Undergrip	8-12	2

Calves

Exercise	Reps	Sets
Calf Raise	15-25	3

Abdomen

Exercise	Reps	Sets
Crunches	As many as possible	3

Cool-down

Exercise	Time
Any Cardio Machine	10 minutes

2nd Week's Training

Warm-up

Exercise	Time
Any Cardio Machine	10-15 minutes

Legs/Bottom

Exercise	Reps	Sets
Leg Curls	10-12	3
Leg Extensions	10-12	3
Adductors	12	3
Kick Backs	8-12	3

Backs

Exercise	Reps	Sets
Lat Pulls	8-12	3
Hyperextensions	15-25	1

Chest

Exercise	Reps	Sets
Inclined Bench Press	8-12	3

Shoulders

Exercise	Reps	Sets
Behind the Neck Press	8-12	3

Triceps

Exercise	Reps	Sets
Narrow Grip Bench Press	10-12	2

Biceps

Exercise	Reps	Sets
Barbell Curl	10-12	2

Calves

Exercise	Reps	Sets
Calf Raise	15-25	2

Abdomen

Exercise	Reps	Sets
Twisted Crunch	As many as possible	2

Cool-down

Exercise	Time
Any Cardio Machine	10 minutes

Maximal Strength Training

Duration: 4 weeks; following muscle building training

Loading: 85-95% of max
No single reps!

Warm-up

Exercise	Time
Ergometer (not stepper)	10-15 minutes

Legs

Exercise	Reps	Sets	Load
Squats or	12	1	Easy
Leg Press	8	1	Moderate
	3-5	3	Heavy

Back

Exercise	Reps	Sets	Load
Seated Row	12	1	Easy
(Only when apparatus	8	1	Moderate
with upper body	3-5	1	Heavy
support avail.)			

Alternative:
Lat Pulls

Chest

Exercise	Reps	Sets	Load
Bench Press	12	1	Easy
	8	1	Moderate
	3-5	3	Heavy

Shoulders

Exercise	Reps	Sets	Load
Behind the Neck Press	12	1	Easy
	8	1	Moderate
	3-5	3	Heavy

Abdomen

Exercise	Reps	Sets
Crunches	As many as possible	2
Reverse Crunches	As many as possible	2

Cool-down

Exercise	Time
Any Cardio Machine	10 minutes

Recovery Training

Duration: During the playing season when you cannot do intensive strength training workouts

Loading: 40-50% of max
(recreational athletes)
60% of max
(experienced athletes)

Warm-up

Exercise	Time
Any Cardio Machine	10-15 minutes

Legs

Exercise	Reps	Sets
Leg Curls	8	2
Leg Extensions	8	2
Adductors	8	2

Back

Exercise	Reps	Sets
Seated Row	8	2
Lat Pulls	8	2

Chest

Exercise	Reps	Sets
Bench Press	8	2

Shoulders

Exercise	Reps	Sets
Lateral Deltoid Raise	8	2

Triceps

Exercise	Reps	Sets
Triceps Press Down	12	1

Biceps

Exercise	Reps	Sets
Dumbbell Curl	12	1

Calves

Exercise	Reps	Sets
Calf Raises	15-25	2

Abdomen

Exercise	Reps	Sets
Crunches	As many as possible	2

Cool-down

Exercise	Time
Any Cardio Machine	10 minutes

In Focus

ISOMETRIC MUSCLE TRAINING

Beginners in particular can benefit from isometric strength training exercises. This type of training became popular in the 1970s and involves the static contraction of muscles with a constant joint angle. One example of this is holding the dumbbells at right angles when training the biceps. The weight selected is high enough so that the position can be held for no longer than 6-8 seconds with maximum effort.

The advantage of static training is that, for many exercises, no dumbbells or other apparatus are required. For example, chest and arm muscles can be trained by pressing the hands together in different ways or against stable objects (walls, door frames, etc.). This training can be refined still further by using dumbbells. Many so-called intensive methods are hybrids that are more or less similar to isometric training. If you really concentrate on using maximum effort, this is a relatively streamlined and quick training method.

However, isometric training is no magic wand. The disadvantages are primarily a loss of muscle elasticity and the potentially dangerous stress it puts on the cardio-vascular system. This can be counteracted by a good breathing technique and a balanced combination of static and dynamic exercises.

SUMMARY

- Vary the exercises

- Alternate between the different training programs

- Use the complete range of movement in each exercise

- Always ensure you perform each exercise correctly

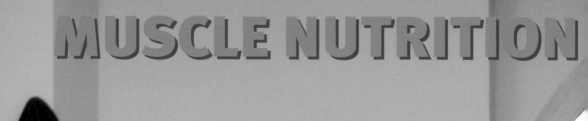

MUSCLE NUTRITION

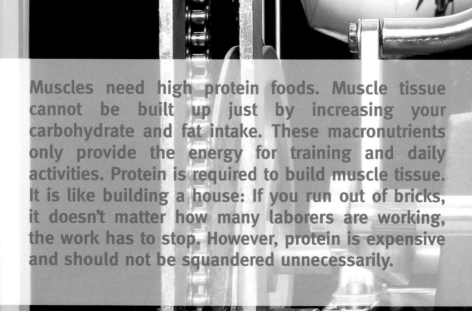

Muscles need high protein foods. Muscle tissue cannot be built up just by increasing your carbohydrate and fat intake. These macronutrients only provide the energy for training and daily activities. Protein is required to build muscle tissue. It is like building a house: If you run out of bricks, it doesn't matter how many laborers are working, the work has to stop. However, protein is expensive and should not be squandered unnecessarily.

Even though the aim of weight training is to gain strength, the training itself involves deliberately damaging muscle tissue. In order to get stronger and increase the amount of muscle tissue, cells must first be broken.

The modern game of soccer places great demands on the player's conditioning levels.

The modern game of soccer demands a high level of conditioning. We often hear commentators or coaches saying that a player or even the whole team has run out of strength before the end of the game. Strength is certainly needed in team sports – we have already seen that in this book – but when players run out of steam, it is not strength that they lack but endurance.

According to nutrition science, endurance depends mainly on the optimal intake of carbohydrate-rich foods. Bread, pasta, rice, vegetables and fruit provide this, as do all sugar-containing foods.

Nutrition Tip

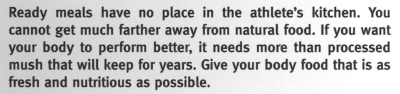

Ready meals have no place in the athlete's kitchen. You cannot get much farther away from natural food. If you want your body to perform better, it needs more than processed mush that will keep for years. Give your body food that is as fresh and nutritious as possible.

Fat also provides energy: per ounce, sugar provides nearly twice as much as carbs. It takes a lot of training before the process of extraction of energy from fats works optimally though. Regular, ultra-long endurance loads are required, which soccer players never do.

This fat intake is very important for Marathon runners and triathletes, but for team sports, an excessive fat intake has a negative impact on physical condition. Particularly when carbohydrates and large amounts of fat are combined in a meal, the carbohydrate metabolism is negatively impacted. Spaghetti Bolognese is a bad choice for the ambitious soccer player, at least during the season. The way round this is to cook it yourself and use low-fat ingredients where possible. If you prepare the Bolognese sauce with tartar and a little olive oil, the fat content will naturally be reduced. But you eat in the restaurant or at your Mum's, the same care will probably not be taken!

> When carbs and excessive fat are combined in a meal, there is a negative effect on the metabolism.

SUPER-FOOD FOR MUSCLES

Any form of muscle activity requires energy, which must constantly be replaced, as the body's own "gas tanks" are limited, at least as far as carbohydrates, the superfuel, are concerned. About 10.5-12.5 ounces (300-350 grams) can be stored as glycogen, the storage form of carbohydrates. However, with improved conditioning and a carbohydrate-rich diet, theoretically this storage capacity can be approximately doubled.

But how do muscles obtain energy from carbs? In every muscle cell there is a reserve of stored carbohydrate in the form of a little grain of glycogen. These reserves are filled with blood sugar via the blood circulation. In normal daily life, this system is always able to supply enough energy.

Low-fat ingredients can drastically reduce the fat content of pasta dishes like ravioli.

With regard to carbohydrate intake during loading, unless the load is of extremely long duration, the immediate effect on the energy reserves will be negligible. However, drinking fluids with a sugar content of less than 8% can benefit performance. These drinks prevent a premature fall in blood sugar levels and the resultant reduction in coordination and concentration.

Nutrition Tip

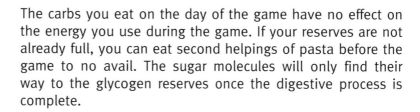

Even under heavy loading, the body cannot easily absorb more than 1.7 pints of fluid per hour. During the game, that is only possible during the half-time break, in spite of the many short stoppages. As even small fluid losses clearly diminish performance levels, about 0.4-0.8 pints of fluid should be drunk before the game starts.

The carbs you eat on the day of the game have no effect on the energy you use during the game. If your reserves are not already full, you can eat second helpings of pasta before the game to no avail. The sugar molecules will only find their way to the glycogen reserves once the digestive process is complete.

CARBOHYDRATES

One doesn't need to be a nutrition scientist to know that the sugar in soda or candy does not have the same beneficial effect on performance levels as the sugar in fresh fruit. To understand the different reactions our bodies have to different sources of carbohydrates, we must take a look behind the scenes of our bodies' complex metabolic processes.

Low-sugar drinks prevent a premature fall in blood sugar levels and the resultant reduced coordination and concentration.

Compared to complex carbohydrates, mono and disaccharides are often dismissed as bad. The reason for this is that more complex sugar molecules, like those found as starch in whole grain products, pass more slowly and steadily from the intestine to the bloodstream than simple ones like glucose, thereby avoiding excessive insulin spikes.

Complex carbohydrates raise blood sugar levels only moderately and do not cause excessive insulin spikes.

However, things are not quite so simple in practice. For example, normal household sugar – a disaccharide, composed of one glucose and one fructose molecule – is considered to be rather harmless with regard to its effect on blood sugar levels, as the negative effect of the glucose is canceled out by the positive effect of the fructose. If household sugar can be reproached for anything, it is that it consists of empty calories. The fructose in fruit is also a monosaccharide. However, this should not stop anyone from regularly helping themselves from the fruit bowl.

Instead of wondering how many carbohydrate molecules a particular food item contains, or going shopping with lists of the glycemic indices as a guide to separating foods into good and bad, it is better to orient your daily diet toward a target that applies to everything you eat: eat as naturally as possible. The more preparation steps that food goes through before it ends up on your plate, the less value it has.

The ingredients of vegetables, such as vitamins, are largely conserved by suitable preparation, such as steaming.

The body of a hard-training athlete is not just entitled to be satisfied at mealtimes but to be nourished with the best that nature can offer. The guiding principle when preparing food is therefore as much as necessary, as little as possible. As we are now hundreds of thousands of years away from living in the wild, raw meat is indigestible for most people. So I don't mean that you have to become a raw-food fanatic or devour raw steak. But vegetables should not be overcooked or drowned in heavy sauces; they should be steamed to preserve their vitamin content.

Raw vegetable salads also largely preserve the important ingredients of the vegetables. Products should of course also be purchased as freshly and as near as possible to preparation time. Preserved food should be the absolute exception. The best alternative to fresh produce is frozen foods. Contrary to popular belief, modern frozen foods even contain nutrients like air soluble vitamins in almost completely preserved amounts.

Food should be bought as fresh and as near to preparation time as possible.

EATING RIGHT

The comparison with automobile fuel clarifies already that the absolute carbohydrate intake should be closely connected to consumption. So in soccer, playing ability and training effort are decisive. Someone who trains two or three times a week and sits on the substitutes' bench on the weekend naturally needs fewer carbohydrates than someone who trains twice a day and plays the full 90 minutes every weekend. In intensive training, the carbohydrate requirement can climb to over 1 ounce per 11 lb of bodyweight. For a player weighing 165 lb., that means at least 15 ounces of carbs per day. Older players can manage with 9-10.5 ounces of carbohydrates.

If you do not benefit from a sports science back-up team that calculates your energy needs for you, you just need to check the scales every day. Any losses or gains in weight always indicate an energy intake that is either too high or too low for your needs.

Carbohydrate nutrition is often inadequate, firstly because too much fat is consumed, and secondly because it is not so easy to eat several hundred of "healthy" carbs grams a day. All starch-containing foods like pasta, rice and bread are important, preferably the whole grain varieties.

There is some consolation for those who think that the exclusive consumption of whole grain foods is only for health freaks: after a hard workout, something sweeter is required. An insulin spike is now desirable. The depleted cells now urgently need to replace the nutrients used up during the workout and are therefore particularly receptive for several hours afterwards.

Soccer players should go for the whole grain versions of starchy foods like bread.

STRENGTH TRAINING FOR SOCCER

The nutrients circulating in the bloodstream are dependent on insulin in order to reach the cells. You can eat an ice-cream or a piece of cake after working out without feeling guilty. You shouldn't do this before the game though. The energy boost this gives you soon disappears, long before the end of the game or the work-out.

Post workout treats are definitely allowed, as the nutrients in the blood necessary for recovery are dependent on insulin.

Nutrition Tip

Whole grain oat flakes are a first-class source of energy for tired muscles. Along with large amounts of carbohydrate (nearly 60g per 100g) and vegetable protein, they are also rich in minerals that bring important trace elements like potassium and magnesium, and also vitamins that are so important for muscle activity.

Top soccer players can also reach for a nutritional supplement. While amateur players already start feeling peckish under the shower, this feeling eases more and more as the training intensity increases. However, it is in top level soccer that the rapid replenishment of the nutrient reserves is particularly important. It is the time required for recovery that determines how soon the next workout can be done with the best result. As these supplements can be dissolved in fluids and drunk, they can even be consumed when you are not feeling hungry. Nutritional supplements also contain calories that must, of course, be considered as part of the total energy intake.

Nutrition Tip

PROTEIN
– THE BUILDING BLOCK

An insufficient protein intake jeopardizes strength and overall performance.

Protein is the building block required to build nearly every cell in the body. Someone who trains intensively first needs more protein and secondly uses up more protein-containing tissue, which must replaced as soon as possible after the workout. An insufficient protein intake always jeopardizes strength levels and general performance levels. The immune system can also suffer from a lack of protein.

Admittedly, the amount of protein consumed is less important than the range of amino acids it contains. Protein is just the collective term for completely different classifications of amino acids. In general, our bodies react quite badly to the intake of "foreign" proteins. When ingested in the form of food, the protein is split up immediately. The smaller the chains that enter the blood stream, the easier it is for our bodies to deal with them. These short-chain amino acids are called peptides.

A maximum of five chained amino acid molecules can be absorbed from the intestine into the bloodstream. This is why care is needed when complex protein chains are sold as some kind of magic bullet. It is much more important to consume sufficient quantities of the amino acids most required by the body. It can then use these to build the necessary chains itself.

As with carbohydrates, the quality of the protein source is important. Meat is better than sausages and frankfurters, fish is better than fish cakes and natural milk products are better than those "improved" by adding sugar, flavoring and coloring.

If the body is supplied with sufficient quantities of the most important amino acids, it can build the proteins itself.

Nutrition Tip

As far as ingredients are concerned, eggs are better for you than they are said to be. Their protein content is particularly high. Be careful when buying them though; eggs are already a week old when they go into your shopping cart, which dangerously increases their content of bacteria and salmonella. It is therefore better to buy eggs directly from the producer.

Performance-oriented soccer players should consume a total of about 1 ounce of protein per 41 lbs of bodyweight per day. That means about 4 ounces per day for a man weighing 165 lb. That is not so different from normal consumption anyway. The source should be different though, for many sources of protein come with a whole array of saturated fatty acids, of which the body can actually only use a few, for example to build hormones. Most are used to produce energy. The requirement is already met by carbohydrates though. Adding large amounts of fat would be like filling a tank with super gas and then adding normal gas on top.

As in the case of the car, the superfluous energy just overflows and ends up around the stomach, hips and thighs.

Part of our protein requirements come from vegetable sources that also provide carbohydrates, such as bread or pasta. The high quality animal proteins should be eaten with as little fat as possible, e.g., poultry, skim milk, produce and fish.

TOTALLY FAT-FREE?

Of course, you don't need to eliminate every single ounce of fat from your diet. That is not only unnecessary, but dangerous for your health. The body definitely needs fat, at least mono-unsaturated fats like those in olive oil and Omega-3 fatty acids as found in salmon, mackerel or grape seed oil. It is a good idea to eat fish twice a week, especially oily cold-water fish. Olive oil can be used any time a vegetable oil is required.

The fats you should eliminate are saturated fats, which essentially provide only energy that we do not require in our modern lifestyles, not even as hard-training soccer players. Superfluous saturated fats not only make us fat and create undesirable "problem areas," but they can also make us sick in the long term. So, limit your fat intake to 20% of your total calorie intake.

Edible oils contain the monounsaturated fats that our bodies require.

The U.S. government advises a limit of 30%, but the remaining 10% should be saved for foods that really boost your performance, such as carbs and proteins.

Nutrition Tip

Soccer players and other athletes need increased supplies of antioxidants, e.g., vitamins C, E and betacarotenoids, or trace elements like Selenium. The high oxygen uptake during workouts subjects athletes to a great deal of oxidative stress. Antioxidants provide considerable protection against the resulting free radicals.

A COUPLE OF BEERS AFTER THE GAME

Another word on the subject of alcohol: For many fans, alcohol is as much a part of soccer as their team's scarf and banner. There is no harm in celebrating an unexpected victory or the end of the seaso. However, someone who regularly drinks more than two beers a day is not only eliminating the important mineral magnesium from his body, but also drastically reducing his testosterone levels and endangering his body's ability to recover. Instead of this, you should drink plenty of fluids. Four pints per day is the absolute minimum; on hot training days, your fluid requirement can easily double. Diuretic drinks, like alcohol and coffee, only raise your fluid requirement.

The regular consumption of alcohol can jeopardize the body's ability to recover.

In Focus

NUTRITIONAL SUPPLEMENTS

Proteins, branched amino acids, carbohydrates and vitamins, etc., are not only found in foods, but have long been available in the form of nutritional supplements. Opinions are divided as to the value of these supplements. There are doctors and sports scientists who say they can increase performance levels, but there is also a rather conservative group that claims that they are unnecessary and prefer to recommend the merits of a balanced diet.

The problem with these opinions is that they have little to do with the athlete's daily life. A player who has not made the jump to the professional game and been fortunate enough to be advised by a nutritional scientist, also has to cope with a hard day's work and family life. That means that his diet is usually just as random as that of a non-athlete. Sufficient proteins or carbohydrates can of course easily be consumed in a conventional diet. This involves worrying about every meal though, leaving nothing out and preparing every item of food so that all the nutrients are retained.

So basically, the issue of nutritional supplements is not really about ideological views or theoretical calculations, but about practical considerations. They can't do miracles; after all, they are not medicines. Protein supplements are usually obtained from milk or soya. But they make the athlete's life easier. However, you should bear in mind that supplements are not a replacement for traditional food, just a complement.

SUMMARY

- Carbohydrates are the most important source of energy for soccer players

- It is best to eat carbohydrates in as natural a state as possible

- Refined sugar and sugared soda drinks have no place in an athlete's diet

- Low-fat sources of protein provide the building blocks for the body's cells

- Monounsaturated fats and Omega 3 fatty acids should not only be part of the soccer player's diet

- Saturated fatty acids mainly provide energy and are unnecessary and even dangerous for the health if the existing carbohydrate intake already meets these energy needs

PHOTO CREDITS

Cover design and Layout: Jens Vogelsang

Cover photo front: dpa Picture-Alliance
back: Yavuz Arslan

All inside photos:
Yavuz Arslan/imageattack

with the exception of:
Adobe Image Library: 30, 43
Dirk Bauer/photoplexus: 118
EyeWire Images: 8, 11, 24, 27
Daniel Kölsche/photoplexus: 31, 116
Life Fitness: 36
Mev Verlag: 113, 115, 122
Pixelquelle.de: 112, 114, 119, 120, 121, 123

Competence in Soccer

Gerhard Frank
Creative Soccer Training

ISBN 978-1-84126-015-0
$ 17.95 US/$ 25.95 CDN
£ 12.95 UK/€ 14.90

Bischops/Gerards
Soccer – One-on-One

ISBN 978-1-84126-013-6
$ 17.95 US/$ 25.95 CDN
£ 12.95 UK/€ 14.90

Erich Kollath
Soccer
Technique & Tactics

ISBN 978-1-84126-016-7
$ 14.95 US/$ 20.95 CDN
£ 8.95 UK/€ 14.90

Bischops/Gerards
Soccer – Warming up
and Warming down

ISBN 978-1-84126-135-5
$ 14.95 US/$ 20.95 CDN
£ 8.95 UK/€ 14.90

Jozef Sneyers
Soccer Training
An Annual Programme

ISBN 978-1-84126-017-4
$ 19.95 US/$ 29.95 CDN
£ 14.95 UK/€ 18.90

Gerhard Frank
Soccer
Training Programmes

ISBN 978-3-89124-556-9
$ 17.95 US/$ 25.95 CDN
£ 12.95 UK/€ 16.90

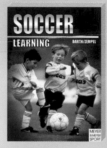

Barth/Zempel
Learning Soccer

ISBN 978-1-84126-130-0
$ 14.95 US/$ 20.95 CDN
£ 9.95 UK/€ 14.90

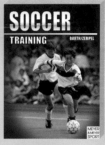

Barth/Zempel
Training Soccer

ISBN 978-1-84126-131-7
$ 14.95 US/$ 20.95 CDN
£ 9.95 UK/€ 14.90

Buschmann/Pabst/Bussmann
Coordination
A New Approach
to Soccer Coaching
ISBN 978-1-84126-063-1
$ 14.95 US/$ 20.95 CDN
£ 9.95 UK/€ 14.90

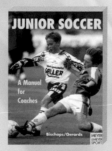

Bischops/Gerards
Junior Soccer
A Manual for Coaches

ISBN 978-1-84126-000-6
$ 17.95 US/$ 25.95 CDN
£ 12.95 UK/€ 16.90

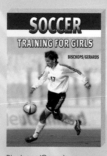

Bischops/Gerads
Soccer Training
for Girls

ISBN 978-1-84126-097-6
$ 17.95 US/$ 25.95 CDN
£ 12.95 UK/€ 16.90

Bischops/Gerards/Wallraff
Soccer Training for
Goalkeepers

ISBN 978-1-84126-186-7
$ 16.95 US/$ 24.95 CDN
£ 12.95 UK/€ 16.95

MEYER & MEYER... the Sport Publisher
sales@m-m-sports.com • www.m-m-sports.com

MEYER
& MEYER
SPORT